THE BOY FROM UNDER THE TREES

DON WASHBURN

The Poet's Press
PITTSBURGH, PA

Copyright © 2012 by Don Washburn
All Rights Reserved
Second printing, 2017

This is the 199th publication of
THE POET'S PRESS
2209 Murray Avenue #3
Pittsburgh, PA 15217-2338
www.poetspress.org

ISBN 0-922558-66-3

CONTENTS

WAKINGS 7
WELLSPRINGS 13
WINDFALLS 19
WONDERS 25
WINDOWS 31
WEATHERS 37
WHETSTONES 43
WORLDLINGS 49
WALLS 55
WREATHS 61
WOODCUTS 67
WARNINGS 73
WRAITHS 78
WHISPERS 85
WEBS 91
WICKS 97

ABOUT THE POEMS 103
ABOUT THE POET 104
ABOUT THE BOOK 106

WAKINGS

1

Ding dong, dingdong, dingdong bell,
ring the dark sleep we rise from,
ring the day's light where we dwell,
ring and bring in kingdom come.

Swing and tell how now we wake,
foresee, fulfill, and forsake
morning's sun song, evening's knell.
Ding dong, dingdong, dingdong bell.

2

Paint a water-color sky,
a haze of maples, and beneath
the tangled neighborhoods that lie
transubstantiate as breath.

And in this nook of time define
gable, gate, grackle, grapevine,
the countless exactitudes of place,
And at the window pane, my face.

3

And I awoke in that timeless room,
whose providence I knew by heart:
the papered walls were in full bloom,
and the ceiling unfolded like a chart.

The house downstairs, hearty with light,
door by door unlocked my sight;
and the sun, exploding in the street,
spread a fiery carpet at my feet.

4

Sparrow street, wheel-barrow street,
windows like faces in a dream.
Hazy in the summer heat,
things become the things they seem.

Sparrow street, narrow street,
chirping voices and flying feet.
Around me here, like wings are swirled
intimations of my first world.

5

I remember riding to Christmas high
on my father's shoulder, hooded in a green
blanket — dazzled in the darkness by
the scent and sense of things unseen.

Beguiled by the sweet conspiracy,
I breakfasted on light and rose to see
what presence filled the plentiful room,
making the winter morning bloom.

6

These disorderly neighborhoods
address me without hesitation
like urchins. Each turning alludes
to some suspended conversation.

Free as an imbecile, I eavesdrop
on sparrows and sunporches. Or I stop
to see what an unkempt garden discloses.
Loitering, I gather poems like roses.

7

Long, how long I lay in the grass
one summer night and looked high
into the heaven's dark looking-glass,
dusty with light, far as the eye

could see — stars, and stars behind
the stars, without end — staring to find
in all that unreflecting space
a face to fathom my own face.

8

I am the boy from under the trees.
The hours, like clouds, go drowsing by.
Wonder enough I find in these
slow funerals of earth and sky.

In a heaven of leaves the summer dies.
Rooted in earth, the dead will rise.
I am the boy from under the trees,
learning by heart these mysteries.

wellsprings

9

Night wind, cool and dark,
offers up the cup of being.
Dawn wind whets the spark
which makes bright our winnowing.

Noon wind unwinds a world
where our destinies are furled.
Westering wind whispers of sleep,
a sleep where all our wisdoms keep.

10

The Twins unbound the morning sun,
easing the intellect and the tongue.
Kindling a hearth on the pink horizon,
the Crab twitched his moody tong.

The white moon, balancing in the Scales,
crooned of radiance and grails.
Thus constellated, did my birth rehearse
dispositions of universe.

11

I came from a bottomless well, a drink
drawn from one bibulous draft
of being. I know nothing of Nothing-
ness, only the rush of sense, the quaffed

light, lively in my ken. How might
fountains of insight or second sight
make brighter that plenary origin?
Without beginning, it all began.

12

"Choose these workaday people,"
The angel said, "and their homely decencies.
Vices abound. The sow of evil
feeds on its farrow. Trust to their mercies

and envy no rich man's son.
They will free you, strong in the run
of the world. Eat their coarse bread
And be hearty." And so I did.

13

Brother, we are to one another
charmed sailors who navigated
the lathering shoals and beached together
where uncharted patrimonies waited.

Learn with me the indigenous language,
this climate's history of joy and anguish,
and hunt in the uplands of our heritage
treasure for another voyage.

14

Element, ambience, mother, and more:
pia mater to my mortal chord,
abundant cotyledon for
my umbilical stumble sunward.

Mana, manna, mother, and host,
your oven ordained and your roast,
shower of aliment to content
firmament and fundament.

15

My father wound and set his life
exactly — like a railroader's watch.
His every train of thought arrived
on schedule. Caution cleared the tracks.

God save him for the pains he took
to bring us safe. But there are track-
less lines, untraveled, where no clocks run,
stations and destinations unknown.

16

Feeling, godmother at my birth,
aunt, ruth of childlessness, tell
me was it you who touched me with unearth-
ly expectation? And what strange spell

summoned the eschatological host
that perfumed the rose garden of your ghost-
ly hope? May you bloom with them
in some splendiferous Jerusalem.

Windfalls

17

Husked from our tight houses, elat-
ed, we fly in the fields, and our wanderings
settle us among milkweeds to celebrate
the rite of cracking open things.

The ripe birds, shredded, bleed
white blood and unfeather each seed,
to blow like clouds in the slow day
and follow us, floating, every which way.

18

We packed a lunch and climbed the humped
wood. Rank thickets scourged us as we bent
along the paths. The green flies jumped.
We breathed thick sun on the long ascent,

but at the springs we sat in the shade
and listened to the music the waters made.
On the cool rocks it dripped like jewels.
We drank at the fern scented pools.

19

In the vegetable dusk fire-flies
blink on, blink off. Our fingers dredge
the air, and our phosphorescent eyes
flicker in every thicket and hedge.

Children of the summer night
that gathers us, we gather light,
and homeward carry in fragile jars,
a universe of dying stars.

20

At my feet the blushing nakedness
of the unnested bird. And I marvel how
the delicate blue veins of a princess
marble her limp neck, obedient now.

Like attentive gallants, quickly
the sparking flies gather, and thickly
sue the virginal flesh with kissings,
making green capes of their wings.

21

We imagined the mausoleum was where
Old Man Death had his house, and deep
inside he waited. And by day slept there,
the same sleep the dead sleep,

but might be awakened if we should dare
to rattle the iron gate, or to stare
through the stained-glass window, or shout
his name — half afraid he might come out.

22

Like soaked punk, the drowned kitten
floats, yellow and hairy, pug
nose up. The fat entrails are hidden
beneath lily pads. The smile is smug.

Summer rain pocks and grooves
the surface. Slowly the kitten moves,
making indolent designs among
the prim, white blossoms on the pond.

23

We followed the spur in weedy tracts
out beyond the last paved street,
tripping on tiptoe the rusty tracks
and leaping the ties with giant feet.

No engines came. We never could hear
the iron rumbling in one cold ear.
But tracks go somewhere. So we spent
whole mornings to see where they went.

24

The luminous cherries are ripe again,
carmine stars in a leaf-green sky,
Beaks burgeon where our moths had been.
Our arms grow feathery and fly.

Though witches lurk to scold or chase
us, perching, we darken that leafy space,
spit pits all morning, grow dissolute,
feasting like blackbirds on the tart fruit.

WONDERS

25

At hide and seek among the firs
in the dark churchyard, I lay still
and heard the wordless universe
hunting me along the long hill.

Among the needles, under the black
belfry and wintry zodiac,
I was discovered and came home
to a silence deeper than my own.

26

Skittish tomboy, somebody's kid
sister skidding on the ice
and trailing bright red scarves amid
the wintry sunburst, turned twice

as I passed and with a shy smile
showed me what was all the while
waiting, frozen in the virginal air,
to turn that blustery weather fair.

27

In my mother's cradle Neptune sang,
god of the salt breezes and the lobster's
claw, whose glaucous chargers sprang
to our horizon. And like worshippers,

newly awake to the quake of the steep
breakers, we exulted in the deep
commotion of that enormous motion,
of ocean, ocean, ocean, ocean!

28

No need to thank that intercessor,
forgotten now, whose sesame flung
open those ageless pages. My treasure
it was, soon or late. And among

wonders, words swaying like houris,
on a carpet woven of allegories,
drunk with the wine of Khayyam, I
went flying with the All-Seeing-Eye.

29

Katzenjammers tipped over the clouds,
dousing the pate of creation. The tin
roof drummed. Uproarious in gutters and spouts,
a tippler babbled to be let in.

Noses pressed to the saving glass,
we held at bay the pratfall chaos,
and only our eyes, straining to see,
flashed in the dark our secret glee.

30

Carnival organ, musty tunes,
music rank as the sweat of man,
humorless freaks, bloated balloons,
faces old when the world began.

The stripper's lips purse and pout.
Wheels are spinning as luck runs out.
Carnival organ, colored light:
Ancient music on a summer night.

31

Praise the shoulder-cushioning grass,
where, ball-like, bouncing, we fell down,
the blades pricking our necks, the crass
ground staining us green and brown.

Praise the fields where like colts we romped,
unlimbered our legs, sprinted and stomped,
the breath in our lungs unspeakably sweet,
and the earth alive under our feet.

32

So scattered the word-drunk rhyme-
sters (my mnemonic ilk), these pre-
cincts might forget, save that I'm
correspondent to their mortality.

Scrupulous of serendipities,
I memorize what moments please,
lest alien scribblers fail to note,
or grow careless, or misquote.

windows

33

Shadow, sun-splash, shimmer, shade:
poplars blink in my side-long eye.
Schoolrooms are murmuring, the staid
Voices afloat in the flowing sky.

At the desks the lessons are dinned,
but wordless in that window's wind,
poplars darken, poplars grow bright,
fluent with the drift of light.

34

One window on this quiet street
drowns my eyes like a shadowy pool:
Leaves engulf the window seat.
The unseen room is green and cool.

Who lurks, I wonder, behind the sill?
What Scylla, submersible and still,
tending dim grottos of oblivion,
though children of the sun peer in?

35

Like astronomers, we hunched at the edge
of the pond's green prism, angling to see
galaxies of algae, the nebulous flotage
of bubble-flux, frog-jelly, and flocculi.

Among the plasms and planets of pollywog,
we scanned the yeasty bottom, agog
for wonders and whatever hurled
the spark that spawned that watery world.

36

The stairwell to the footbridge stank
of urine. And its black throat was limed
with an excrement of words. In the dank
coal dirt we strangled as we climbed.

But at the last landing, the sky
opened, clear and limitless. And high
above the river the long bridge swung,
and the winds were sweet that we walked among.

37

Now the lawns of the rich are mysterious moats, affluent with the liquid dusk. One lamp post in the distance glows, quaint and chivalric.

Beyond the wrought-iron gates and ornate hedges, people of the manor
pass at their pleasure. So strangely far it is from here to where they are.

38

Bottled in their neon caves, they rant and rumble. No scent of women here. Oaths explode. The air is militant, spoiling of cigars and stale beer.

Belly to belly at cards they brawl harmlessly. Thick throats guffaw,
or, sotted and ponderous, settle indoors innumerable arguments and wars.

39

On fire with fever, I floated high
in my darkened bedroom, undismayed
by sleep or the slow June gone by
at the faint edges of the drawn shade.

And inklings only, a flutter of wings,
whispered to me of shifting things
below—how the weathering window grew
hermetic, and the crystal sun withdrew.

40

Death's old woman does house-keeping,
swinging her broom, making room,
heartless of heartbeats, sweeping, heaping,
dust in the brain, dust in the tomb.

Spry and sprightly, her spring cleaning –
fall away flesh – fall away meaning –
hurries remains to the rubbish heap.
At her window pane the unborn peep.

WEATHERS

41

Thunderheads spout, blitzing creation,
Sudden invasion of sprouts and shoots.
Buds, tumbling in the ventilation,
puff and spray like parachutes.

At large again to the charging earth,
we listen. Shrill explosions of mirth
reincorporate the children, raucous
corporals to a banzai of crocus.

42

The warm winds blow the season in:
clouds, swollen, soak the earth.
In pulpy showers, green and flaxen
underfoot, the trees give birth.

In a liquid world all things flow
earthward, skyward, high and low.
Even the hunchback girl floats by,
lips cupped, distance in her eye.

43

In the equilibrium that comes
when summer, plumb as a stilled
pendulum, temporizes, thrums
with heaviness, and is filled

with long noons, humming with sun,
centered and at rest, I am one
at one with something, with nothing then
to tick me into time again.

44

Radios, seasonal as a sultry day,
dial the solstice as it nears:
crowds crackle and the play-by-play
curves endless innings in our ears.

Our stars, like zodiacs, swing around,
and to the ritual of that sound,
epic and orderly, we resume
immortal summer and are home.

45

Which of your dutiful deputies
calls at the court of the August sun,
seeking an audience, if you please,
with immanent eminence, noon begun,

and hearing a lordly cicada chirr,
a cheerful charter, as it were,
enunciates most faithfully
this summery summary? Envoy: me.

46

We leap into this bonfire heap
of crackling leaves, pungent as smoke,
stoking the furnaces that keep
the seasons sane. And, trusting in a cloak

that rustles with these rusts, we brave
the pyrogenic mulch, the grave
composts where salamanders swarm.
Shoot up again without harm!

47

On the counter rows of false-faces
stared at us with lidless eyes.
We recognized those gnomish races,
fitting ourselves to each disguise.

Next day the cold, clear morning world
made us forget. But windows were whorled
with soap. And we found in every crack
the tell-tale confetti, orange and black.

48

Specks, flecks, flakes, float,
flit, skitter, scud in the sky,
flutter, flurry, cloud remote
slopes, slicken, thicken, to lie

down, downy, soundless towns,
toward deep dawns that bounce
our blown beds, fill heads
with hills, spill sped sleds.

WHETSTONES

49

Schoolbells harvested us like wheat,
wild in the windrow lanes. Blythe
laughter was blowing us, tasseled and sweet
in the morning sun. Snick of the scythe!

Ricked in this same field of years,
together we sat, all eyes and ears.
The rooms gave our faces a single life,
mowed in time by a single knife.

50

These rolls restore Avalon in
my ears and that first company
of peers, rostered from oblivion,
punctual enlistment, eager to be.

Dragon, lend me your breath of flames.
I salute that Pendragon of names
who entitled each plausible face.
In a scribble of voices I take my place.

51

What did we learn in school today?
Even the straightest line can skew.
A lie may have its sidelong way.
Words are a trapdoor to fall through.

From a pit of smiles rage may leap.
In a crack in the wall a dream can keep.
Clocks have hands, but do not play.
We learned all this in school today.

52

All week the feathery valentines
fluttered in the crimson box like doves.
We waited, listening. The cooing rhymes
ballyhooed our balloted loves.

The flocks flew out, hitting each mark
like arrows. Targeted we learned the stark
lesson: love is nested with small reason.
And no bird augurs the heart's treason.

53

Harry Swick, not very quick,
seldom got the hang of it.
His thinking was a little thick,
short of words, short of wit.

But Harry grew to quite a size,
which made him wiser in our eyes.
And when we found out what he meant,
his stammering was eloquent.

54

Molly Manners, "Little Dutch Girl,"
chubby, giggly and so sweet,
made her letters curve and curl.
The teacher thought it very neat.

Molly Manners knew how to spell.
None of us could do so well.
There at the head of the class she stood,
although her head was made of wood.

55

MISS CRAWLEY, LIBRARIAN the plaque
forewarned. Behind the marble desk
she sat, fierce as Cerberus, her back
to the cave of books. I went unblessed.

But, Odyssean, I won the farther
shore, jubilant in that other
kingdom, consorting with the dead,
forgetful of time in the time I read.

56

When Miss Prendergast, our principal, died,
we were resurrected in the April air,
marched from the stale rooms, bright-eyed
and sociable, to view her somewhere.

In the parlor, with her starched face
prim among lilies and white lace,
we learned a last lesson. Stern is death
and still. Outside we caught our breath.

WORLDLINGS

57

Bruno Hacker had three words he
bespattered you with whenever he spoke.
The first besmirched his Maker's mercy.
Since the second begot him, he abetted the joke

by begetting it at every chance.
The third begat such an awful stench
you hardly believed from what he said
that his behind was not his head.

58

Old Man Sitz had settled ways.
His grocery store was world enough
for him. He stayed put. His days
were a row of cans on a tidy shelf.

You could always find him at his address.
Too much trouble to leave, I guess.
And now in the graveyard he stays put still.
He made the trip but against his will.

59

The roller rink whirrs with their pass-
es. They skirr like gadgets in a galler-
y, their girlish flirtations fatuous and brass-
y, bulls-eyes for some smoking gunner.

Everywhere arms are cocked. The or-
gan booms tunefully. Reeling, they giggle or
grope at their skirts. The banging boys
trophy them away like kewpies.

60

Beast Kochinski was six feet tall,
with a square mouth and a barging walk,
a burly bully who could whip us all.
We never gave him any back talk.

But nobody missed Beast's last fight,
when, backing off, his face turned white,
not fast enough to get away,
or big and mean enough to stay.

61

Rag woman, pushing her carriage, comes
Saturdays to poke among
the ash cans and the rubbish. She hums
to herself a queer little song.

Proud as a new mother, she wheels her
buggy. She couldn't be cheerier.
Are there such precious things in
our ashes and junk, old rag woman?

62

Harlots are hissing on River Street
in doorways and stairwells awash with night.
The shadowy voyagers they greet
vanish in an eddy of colored light.

Harlots are hissing on River Street,
mouths clotted and bittersweet,
selling with their indifferent breath
a touch of life and a touch of death.

63

The Kitchen brothers with their cart
were as strange a pair as you could find.
The crippled one was very smart.
The strong one had a feeble mind.

This one pushed and that one steered.
The cart neither slowed nor veered.
And in an oxymoronic sense,
repaired at once God's negligence.

64

"South Side Josie" had an epic fame
for prodigies of willingness.
The big boys smiled at her name.
They all knew her, more or less.

The siren we imagined was
cinematic and sensuous.
But Josie turned out something less:
a paragon of fecklessness.

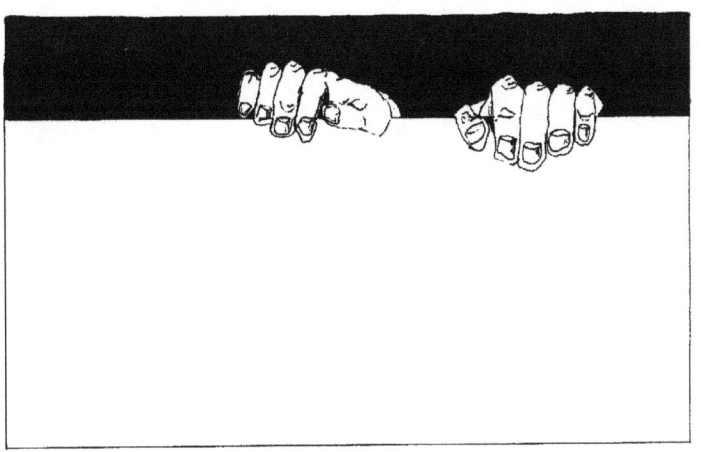

WALLS

65

Behind the counter Miss Harrigan sat,
pregnant with sugar babies, licorice,
and candy hearts, listening to the flat
walls whisper, whisper a stillborn wish.

Neither Norn nor witch, she sold
her penny sweets and grew old.
With yellow eyes sat at her sewing,
watched the children coming, going.

66

Click! And I have her. On the stoop one
old world woman with her black dress.
ankles swollen in the morning sun,
that wrinkled face beyond weariness.

Can she, like a film strip, still whir
back – the black-eyed men dancing her,
laughing? Such nimble feet, she thinks.
Time, that enormous camera, winks.

67

Marie Cuvo, whose hair was red,
lived beside the railroad yard.
The coal dirt silted in her bed.
Her life was colorless and hard.

Marie Cuvo had her pride.
To the rich kids on the other side,
with all their ribbons and gabardine,
she cried, "At least our clothes are clean!"

68

Long, white face, lace, and green eyes
at the window. Her dreams play cat and mouse
with the dark. The antique clock sighs:
tick tock, tick tock. Old maid's house.

Prim cat shapes. They fill her rooms,
her life. She feeds at saucers. The glooms
pounce! The clock runs down. Death scats!
How quickly scattered, Aunt Kate's cats.

69

Alvin Stohl, paladin tall,
what would Quixote say of you,
who would not sally forth at all,
a windmill where no wind blew?

Why, with Dulcinea fled,
did you not follow where she led?
Small reaping for small trouble.
Scarecrow in a field of stubble.

70

In Sonny Boy Johnson's living room
mirrors had cracks and floors were bare.
A weary lamp held back the gloom.
Kerosene smells smudged the air.

But his old mother's ambush eyes
were darkest! Before I could rise
or speak she was gone from the light.
In the broken mirror my face was white.

71

Little Verna with violet eyes
laughs beneath an April moon.
Neither innocent nor wise
she will put on knowledge soon.

Moons will wax and moons will wane,
but she will never be the same.
Where is laughter when it dies,
little Verna with violet eyes?

72

My mother remembers Barbara Kist,
rose-lipped cupid in the faded photos.
first name on the birthday list,
but faithless, so the story goes.

Even so young, I suppose, the heart
has its logic. But for my part,
I do not recall who Barbara kissed
or why it was she was not missed.

WREATHS

73

Kite high on a hill in my hill town
these anecdotal headstones fly
my fancy down the rooftops, down
the steep neighborhoods that lie

buried in sunlight, eventfulness
enough to fill a graveyard. In this
vertical place I tug like a thread
between the living and the dead.

74

Who is this chiseler who writes
such chary numbers in the stone,
a certain sum of days and nights
and then a decimal of bone.

Chip by chip he carves our fates,
limns our lives in a brace of dates.
At the last subtraction our figures rust:
balance of zero, remainder of dust.

75

Winds blow east and winds blow west.
The grey storm clouds assault the sky.
Cypresses have no rest
and grave-flowers are tossed awry.

Weathers of the world dispute
a power dark and absolute.
The dead will neither shudder nor weep,
so deep their sleep, so deep their sleep.

76

She had a summer in the world,
an infant sum of sun and air.
The early roses had unfurled.
The irises were everywhere.

A simple season since her birth,
and here she's added to the earth.
The blossoms, bursting, all are quick
to learn this dark arithmetic.

77

Grave-flowers wither in the sun
and fill the air with sweet decay.
The mourners have risen and gone on.
Now time will have his windy way.

Look! There among the bunches
of white lilies a spider hunches,
his still grey shape inscribed
like a dead face on a tintype.

78

The angel's eyes are white as bone,
and the grey moss stains her weathered cheek.
Death has the smell of crumbling stone
and dry leaves that molder and reek.

In the drift of dust and the rust of rain
carvings blur and lose their grain,
and the very guardians that mark
our going – themselves grow dark.

79

I stopped to muse where a headstone said
in letters mutable and thin
that Musie, eleven, lay long dead
and would not see the sun again.

Her name, muted and far away,
fluttered, flute-like, but could not say
what silences she wandered in
or what the music might have been.

80

The parade ends up at the graveyard,
where tiny flags certify old wars.
The band grows quiet. The honor guard
stands by for prayers and orators.

Then, as the last bars of the anthem die,
they fire seven volleys at the sky.
Somewhere a solitary bugle knells.
Kids scuffle and scramble for the shells.

woodcuts

81

Under pied sycamores we sagged,
lazy in the melding heat,
limbs leaf-heavy, spirits snagged,
the thick roots throttling our feet.

Wreathed in droplets, shaggy with shade,
the body of our breathing made
common cause with summer, and at ease
we dreamed our mottled dreams like trees.

82

Sacred to exuberance,
the far-flung maple trees fly
their winged seed. Squadrons, danc-
ing in the sunlight, dazzle passers-by.

As prodigal, we pause to paste
samaras on our noses, and, thus graced,
lift into the day-long wind, to roam
in leafy byways far from home.

83

Liquidamber, whose star-shaped leaves
the wind arranges with innocent art,
you are the most maidenly of trees,
sweet even at the resin heart.

Not so incredible were you to speak
and say, "Before me first that Greek
imagination paused, half
in dream, and heard the dryad laugh."

84

When the paddle-fingered trees spot
the horse-chestnuts, like aggies in
the spread grass, we squint and squat,
popping the whoppers into our tin.

Newly husked from their prickly rinds,
they please our thumbs and ripen our minds
to a roundness. In each fertile nut
we find an eye that does not shut.

85

In wickers of willow light still flows,
light and half-light, shallows and shades
that braid the fading air and compose
chiaroscuros in the arched arcades.

But as evening billows in an indigo arc,
the tangled willows grow slowly dark,
and a spider climbs the west to spin,
web by web, oblivion.

86

Madam Gingko, in a swarm of jade
butterflies, invites the air.
We have savored that tea-dark shade
while twilight combed her windy hair.

Is it she or we who grow abstract
and dream of far places? With tact
that reconciles the yang, the yin,
she gathers even such strangers in.

87

When the Italian peddler knocked
each spring, our pear tree was bent
and thickly knuckled, limbs cocked
in every direction the winter went.

But somehow in his swollen sack
he brought the buds and blossoms back
and left us Mediterranean airs
enough to burnish the backward pears.

88

Nor will this mountain ash be less
than poet among trees, protegé
of the Master Speller and his timeless
spell. What imaginable use to say

that dragon's breath may take the shape
of fruit, mocking the sober grape,
that orange phoenixes still rise
from ashes, if not to rhapsodize?

WARNINGS

89

Abandoned shanties, factories shut
down, shops and outbuildings, unused
sheds, deserted shacks, and huts
can be boarded up, fenced, refused

visitors, plastered with signs that demand
NO TRESPASSING, but a shadowy hand
will deface the walls, shatter the glass
and bring dark larcenies to pass.

90

Crazy houses cannot keep him. Somewhere
over the dark wall, or closer still,
the lunatic lurks at large. His hair
is horrid and his laughter shrill.

Eyes awry and mouth ajar,
he comes to tell you what you are:
something human, something else,
something out of a crazy house.

91

Wet-winged on the porcelain
a filthy blue-fly with a buzz
crawled up the bowl until I ran
floods of water where it was.

I sent it, drowning, down the drain
and did not think to think again,
but heard that river roar all night
and, impaling my dreams, a cry of fright.

92

On the edge of our intentions hide
unpremeditated things,
lunatic shadows that divide
our lives and eclipse our meanings.

When I came that afternoon to find
you, you were already gone. And behind
his window, moonfaced and beguiling,
the half-wit sat, smiling, smiling.

93

Charlie's grandmother, Polish gypsy,
seemed to be a little daft
or maybe occasionally tipsie,
but somehow I never laughed.

Whenever she saw me, with staring eyes,
she volunteered this strange advice:
"Meet a girl, no. You stay apart,
except you love her, all your heart."

94

Bonny White was the teacher's pet,
quiet as a little mouse.
Her clothes were clean as they could get.
She hardly ever left her house.

Bonny White grew so shy
she couldn't look you in the eye.
Now they say that she's gone mad.
Better, I think, if she'd been bad.

95

"R. M. loves D. L." written in chalk
for all to see who pass this way:
tiny poem on the sidewalk,
tiny crocus on an April day.

What is this "love" that all must tell,
though sketchily and not so well?
Chalk of joy on a slate of pain.
Lines erased in the first dark rain.

96

Your world will jerk with a sudden whim
and hurry you down the headlong rails:
faces, turning, diminish and dim;
brakes let go; direction fails.

Oh, do not smile and mistake
that certain time when you will take,
breath choked back in bug-eyed fright,
a rollercoaster into night.

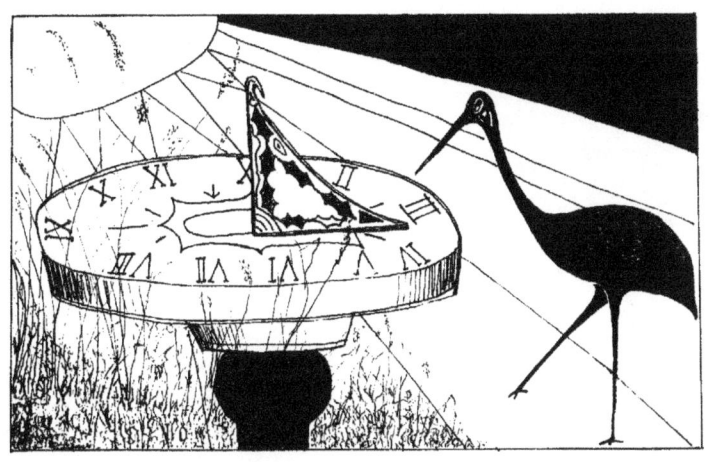

WRAITHS

97

Harold Miller could climb a tree
the very sky was shy to climb,
graceful in that gravity
though apples fell before their time.

Hale as summer, high on a limb,
this is the way I remember him —
though come to earth and long since dead —
still in that tree, still in my head.

98

Down an aisle of uncertain light
I stare. An unkept garden is there,
posthumous as a wreath. Who might
be walking in that faded air?

No one at all. The sundial sleeps
in the tall grass. Each shadow keeps
its slow time. In the rank bowers
there is a ghostly odor of flowers.

99

When Hunker Wallen lost his mind,
he went for a walk to find it again
on legs that left all doubts behind,
following each long street to the end.

By day we would see him in full stride
or bending to search on every side
as though the light, dropped from his face,
lay coin-like in some likely place.

100

Motionless among the rippling graves,
that black crane is an aged crone,
and at her withered shanks laves
a shadowy bottom of earth and stone.

Do her sharp senses fishing the dark,
catch the gleam? Do they remark
the bright fins and the mandala eye?
She jerks. The sun swims in the sky.

101

Where did you fly to, Karl Byrd?
What black mood blotted your black face
without a whimper or a word?
Now we can't find you any place.

Ragamuffins, I thought, were tough
and never knew when they had enough.
If you were dying, nobody heard.
Where did you fly to, Karl Byrd?

102

Sol Richards loved to remember. And on
smoky autumn evenings he would
stop to talk about people long gone
and the old days in the neighborhood.

Sol would not let his histories die.
The dead still danced in his mind's eye.
And they would still be dancing yet,
but death taught Sol how to forget.

103

On the hillside, a white population
of slabs, pillars of salt, undone
with Lot's wife, upright congregation,
patient for the doomsday sun.

So stark still and prim they stand,
in death's aisles a stiff-necked band.
But the parson will sing and dance
    with the strumpet
at the last blast of the last trumpet.

104

Alex Archer played at war
with wooden guns and duffel bags,
and on his harmless sleeves he wore
insignia as bright as flags.

Alex Archer went to war,
but he isn't playing any more.
The guns exploded in his heart,
and all his sleeves have come apart.

whispers

105

Summer's child is gone, elfin Joan,
in whose residence our rough-and-tumble
grew mild, and our ringed faces shone
like sunflowers, attentive and simple.

On the moving day she went, the spell
was broken. And I was alone to tell
how last, in the narrowing light, she turned,
doe-eyed and remote, while autumn burned.

106

The movie palace, drugged with dreams,
ushered my shadow down carpeted
hallways, drifting to half-heard themes.
Archaic lamps glowed poppy-red.

The flowering air, intimate with powers,
held me darkly. In the arcane towers
I floated. A tapestried chamber kept
some imagined princess where she slept.

107

The aspens, adrift in darkness, quake
in the bottomless lane. I listen all night
to the lisp of leaves. In a black lake
the streetlamp floats her sallow light.

Who is it that in this alien wind
slowly descends? My senses are dimmed.
Near, so near, the moonwoman bides,
the opiate eyes, the fingers like tides.

108

Night, a shy girl, beckons with eyes
averted. Past pale streetlamps I float.
The air, lavender with lilacs, lies
heavy. Voices are damped and remote.

There is scarcely a tremor of leaves.
Ghost-like, I pass under the dark eaves.
On a veranda, velvet shadows stir.
Sudden laughter. Silence. Not her.

109

This is the night of the dark-eyed girl,
waiting dreamlike in the crowded hall.
At the moon's white edge the vapors curl.
Time is an eyelash about to fall.

The music is gathering like the sea,
swishing and breathing distantly.
In the high window shadows whirl.
This is the night of the dark-eyed girl.

110

Incendiary in my sight,
she walks. My eyes like dry
tinder burst into light. Each site
is raging and settings rarify.

Long afterwards, inexplicably,
the pale fires quicken. Where she
has passed, pavestones grow luminous
and the narrowest streets, voluminous.

111

My eyes were hunters then and she
the doe. But that uncanny place
devised Diana in her privacy,
the light shooting arrows from her face.

Blind and mindless, I fled that gaze
like a doomed stag. And dying for days
of sudden shapes and feather-swift sounds,
fed my heart to the passionate hounds.

112

Easter is her avatar.
Cameo'd among candles and canticles
she resonates. My devotions are
altered at those aureoles.

In the iconography of her gaze
I divine beatitudes. I praise
the dominions that ring her head.
I too am risen from the dead.

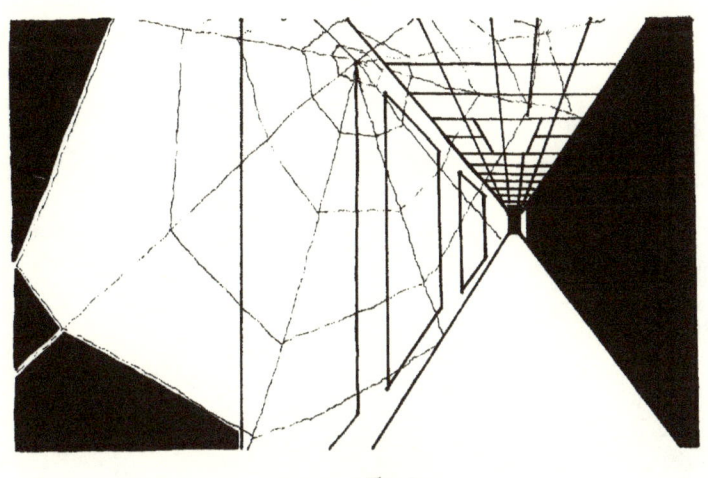

webs

113

She, dark-eyed on the marble sill,
dreams in this autumnal place,
white as an icon and as still,
with shadows on her hair and face.

How gracefully she holds her head,
the light, the dark so subtly wed,
that, pensive as a dying flower,
she beautifies the quiet hour.

114

Though in this passing we are near
enough, and our glances brush
like the tails of comets — though a clear
lens fixes us in a single rush

of light, each felicity defined —
there are far gravities inclined
to whirl us, orbiting, out of reach,
beyond all love, beyond all speech.

115

In a jolting corridor, cheeks ablaze,
Jane strafed me. Her upstart heart,
at hit and run, riddled my daze,
stunting to upset my apple-cart.

Bandit, were I myself again, why
I'd answer your fire and blindly deny
that lovers that come too soon, too late,
must wait upon another fate.

116

I did not kiss you, Rosie Nettle,
though fancies spun us like a bottle,
and, two by two, they tried our mettle
in a game of giggles and tittle-tattle.

At the dark passage we stayed a little,
but I did not kiss you, Rosie Nettle,
too new to labyrinthine perils:
webs of your hair, eyes like candles.

117

Without the slightest splash or dip
of immersion, soundlessly, into the sum-
mer lake blueness of her eyes I slip,
drowsy in those depths and dumb.

And there my inattention swims,
until the flick of an eyelid skims
the surface, washing me back on-
to the sands of conversation.

118

Choruses of girlish levity
linger, a whisper of musk.
Like deer, scenting and skittering, we
are drawn in a net fine as dusk.

At this shy affinity, a goddess
exults. Obediently hunting us,
they quicken their timbrels. Not by chance
we are tamed and tethered to a glance.

119

"What do you have in your lap, shy girl?
What is it that I cannot see?
The folds of your gown wimple and whorl.
What can you be hiding from me?"

"I have for you in my lap, sly boy,
a fabulous apple the color of joy.
The sight will sing in your curious blood,
And a single bite will make you mad."

120

Voices woke me in the dark: wall,
window, patina of the streetlight.
And again, below, the woman, call-
ing, drunk and wanton at midnight.

And something answered her and crept
out of the cavern where I slept,
dropped like a serpent to the earth,
coiled and carnal for her mirth.

wicks

121

It was exactly here we gathered, five
or six under the Saturday sky.
Our dandelion faces blazed. Alive,
we harried suns with our daylong cry.

Suns go down. This is another day.
On the grass the dandelions are grey.
Blow them. The feathery seedlings spill.
In another street small voices shrill.

122

Sheer as a theme of Rachmaninoff,
this dream of befalling time,
unrecoverable, the far off
toccatina of a wind chime.

Occasions lost, inklings given,
December garden in the light of heaven,
strange vicissitudes of grace,
evanescent as a face.

123

Captive in the barber shop
to mirrors and to calendars,
I heard the striking of the strop,
the scissors ticking at my ears.

Risen from that chair, I came
again in time, but not the same.
Another barber, taking years,
trims with a scissors nobody hears.

124

Can I forget you at that last gasp,
my most companionable flesh,
body so near, so dear, whose clasp
is close as blood and breath can mesh?

But membranes burst, members dismembered,
and the electric memories disremembered,
divided by infinity,
what will our old friendship be?

125

Words and words in an endless spout,
great gusts of words, thick as dust,
words and words 'til the sun burns out....
Well, write your words if write you must!

But do not fancy how fine they will look,
emblazoned in that millennial book,
where even the masters, age upon age,
vanish like ink on a yellow page.

126

Write as if to write on stone
words meant for a small place:
poems and monuments are prone
to more than a mortuary space.

Cut with a chisel clean and deep
on such a surface as will keep,
each valediction whole by half,
incisive as an epitaph.

127

When the world is up for cheers like a curtain,
and prompters close their books at last;
when all our lines are said for certain,
and faces fall away like masks....

when, actors, stuffed with too many scenes,
we seek each other behind the screens,
then our hands go round, and in the sound
of God's own laughter we are bound.

128

God plays dawn, and God plays dark.
God plays spider, and God plays fly.
God plays shepherd, and God plays shark.
And God looks out of the lambkin's eye.

God plays you, and God plays me.
God plays all the people we see.
God plays dead, but it's all in fun.
For God and the world and we are one.

About the Poems

These 128 poems in 16 sections are about impressions and events that happened when I was growing up in Easton, Pennsylvania, in the 1940s. As a kid, I was allowed to have the run of my neighborhood. With that freedom, came the excitement of exploration and the joy of discovery. I was left with many memories, moments that still have a special power. The poems are in an eight-line rhyming verse form called the *rispetto*. They sum up what I still keep from these beginnings. I now realize that under the trees of my boyhood I first heard the other-worldly music that was to become a lifelong companion.

About the Poet

Born in 1932, the height of the Depression, Don was the oldest son of Albert and Sylvia Washburn. Albert, a careful, dependable man, worked for the Lehigh Valley railroad most of his life. Sylvia, a feisty redhead, was a stay-at-home mother. Don and his younger brother Ken attended school in their home town of Easton, Pennsylvania, an ethnically mixed, blue-collar city on the Delaware river. Don's first collection of poems — *The Boy From Under the Trees* — explores that world and the excitement of being able to run free in the neighborhoods for whole summers at a time.

A football scholarship to Yale opened the way to his career as a teacher, first in secondary school. Later, with a Ph.D in communication from Denver University, he spent over fifty years in college English departments, teaching an enormous variety of subjects, including literature, speech, semantics, and metaphysics. Since 1971 he has been a professor at the Massachusetts College of Liberal Arts and has made his home in North Adams at the northern edge of the Berkshires. His favorite courses are "The Power of Words," "Science and Spirit," "Rumi's Vision," and "Divine Witness."

During that same period Don, a pliable Geminian, was blessed with five wives (successive, not simultaneous) and four children, a prodigality shared by many in his generation. Relationships with women have always been an important part of his education and continue to this day to lighten up his life. Of course, love is always a risk, one Don has usually been willing to take. The events, however, depicted in his sonnet cycle, *In The Eye of the Red-Tailed Hawk*, have left him somewhat chastened. Even, so, four of his ex-wives are still dear friends — no small achievement. His children and grandchildren, thanks to their mothers, have turned out to be especially gifted in countless ways.

Don has always been a listener of music, mostly classical, but he had never learned an instrument. With the advent of the computer, he discovered that musical illiteracy was no handicap. With the help of Joseph Schillinger's books and several courses with local composers, he taught himself to make music using the Cakewalk Sonar programs, which are the musical equivalent of word processors. Several pieces that have continued to satisfy him are available on his web site, www.donwashburn.com.

In 1980, Don found his way to the Sufi community at New Lebanon, New York, where he began his spiritual studies in the Sufi Order of the West, led then by Pir Vilayat Khan. The Abode of the Message was his home for two years, and he became not only an initiate, but also a *cherag*, someone trained to preside at Universal Worship Services. He also was a member of the first graduating class of the Suluk Academy, then a four-year program in Sufi studies. In his eighties, he still presides at Universal Worship services several times a year. The Sufi experience was invaluable in opening his heart to the reality of God. He has also become a communicant in the United Church of Christ. His most recent collection, *Prayer Beads,* is the harvest taken from these years. The 128 poems are a record of the "wisdom" that the poet, as a perennial seeker, has been able to make his own. But perhaps there is more to come.

The poet observes, "My life has been showered with blessings, so many that it serves to demonstrate how grace trumps error and shortsightedness. Praise be to the One whose mercy makes everything possible."

About the Book

The body type of this book is set in Morris Golden, a font created by William Morris for the Kelmscott Press in 1890. This modern digital recreation of the type by the P22 Type Foundry simulates the soft-edged impression of hand-set metal type on hand-made paper. Morris in turn based his designs on typefaces created by Venetian printer Nicolas Jenson in the 1470s. Prose sections of this book are set in Aldus, a digital typeface inspired by the designs of the great Venetian humanist and publisher Aldus Manutius. Section titles are set in Solemnis, an uncial-style font designed by Günter Gerhard Lange in 1953. Lange created many classic revival fonts for the Berthold foundry, leading that organization through the eras of metal, photo and then digital type design.

The line drawings on the cover and on section titles are by George Jarck, reproduced from the original 1982 limited edition printing of *The Boy from Under the Trees*.

www.ingramcontent.com/pod-product-compliance
Lightning Source LLC
Chambersburg PA
CBHW051658040426
42446CB00009B/1195